Walking with God Through It All

By David Hodges

Walking with God Through It All
Published by Leading Through Living Community LLC

Copyright 2018 by David Hodges

ISBN-13: 978-0-9991308-6-5

Scripture quotations are from the Holy Bible, King James Version (KJV) - www.Bible.com

All Rights Reserved. No part or portion of this publication may be reproduced, stored in a retrieval system, or transmitted in any form or by any means - electronic, mechanical, photocopying, recording, or otherwise - without the express written consent of the author.

For information:
Leading Through Living Community LLC
6790 W. Broad Street
Douglasville, GA 30134

Dedication

I would like to thank my family, all of my sisters and brothers, for taking me in when I needed it the most. Words cannot express the thanks I have in my heart and you all are in my prayers.

And to my brother-laws Lee and Aljay:
May the Lord bless you both richly, and keep you all in His care!

Acknowledgement

I would like to thank
My brother Versia for picking up the ball when I dropped it,
And my sister Annie for stepping in when no one ease understood,
And my sisters Eloise and Velma, the reasons I came to Christ,
And my brother Jesse for his advice and wisdom.

I could go on and on about many people I recognized in the Dedication, but mere words can't express the love I have for all of you.

And Mrs. Lynita Blackwell, my publisher, for this book would not have been possible without her.

Foreword

The Christian journey is a life-long adventure of lessons and discoveries in understanding the rudiments of being one who follows the dictates and teachings of Jesus through the Word of God. David Hodges shares some tasty morsels of scripture to describe his journey into Christianity with an openness and innocence that captures the heart of the reader.

His love for God is juxtaposed by his love for baking. In each instance, the original elements are combined and baked to be transformed into a totally different form. Just as flour mixed with yeast and water becomes bread after baking, an empty, troubled and dejected life become wholesome and fruitful when love, forgiveness, peace, Christ and the Holy Spirit is added to that life.

As the author David Hodges puts it candidly, his longing for truth and the void that he was experiencing, was replaced with love and knowledge of a loving God who will never leave or forsake him. This peaceful and joyous euphoria is only attained when you give your life to accepting and following Jesus Christ.

In its simplicity, this account of the author's life in Christ will warm the heart of the reader, as well as encourage, uplift, and enlighten you if you are experiencing any difficulty in life. If David Hodges can work through alcoholism and schizophrenia to a life of peace and joy, so can you.

Michael David
Resident Pastor
Jubilee Christian Church
International House of God

Introduction

It is answered prayer which brings praying out of the realm of dry, dead things, and makes praying a thing of life and power. It is the answer to prayer which brings things to pass, changes the natural trend of things, and orders all things according to the will of God. It is the answer to prayer which makes praying a power for God and for man, and makes praying real and divine. Unanswered prayers are training schools for unbelief, an imposition and a nuisance, impertinence to God and to man.

Answers to prayer are the only surety that we have prayed aright. What marvelous power there is in prayer! What untold benefits to men does it secure to those who pray! Why is it that the average prayer by the many goes a begging for an answer?

The many of unanswered prayers are not to be solved by the mystery of God's will. We are not the sport of His sovereign power. He is not playing at "make-believe" in His marvelous promise to answer prayer. The whole explanation is found in our wrong praying. We ask and receive not because we ask amiss. If all unanswered prayers were dumped into the ocean, they would come very near filling it. Child of God, can you pray? Are your prayers answered? If not, why not? Answered prayer is the proof of your real praying.

The efficacy of prayer from a Bible standpoint lies solely in the answer to prayer. The benefit of prayer has been well and popularly maximized by the saying, "It moves the arm which moves the universe." To get unquestioned answers to prayer is not only important as to the satisfying of our desires, but is also the evidence of our abiding in Christ. It becomes more important still. The mere act of praying is no test of relation to God. The act of praying may be a real dead performance. It may be the routine of habit. But to pray and receive clear answers, not once or twice, but daily; this is the sure test, and is the gracious point of our vital connection with Jesus Christ.

To God and to man, the answer to prayer is the all-important part of our praying. The answer to prayer, direct and unmistakable, is the evidence of God's being. It proves that God lives, that there is a God, an intelligent being, who is interested in His creatures, and who listens to them when they approach Him in prayer. There is no proof so clear and demonstrative that God exists than prayer and its answer.
The main issues in the Hodges family are alcoholism and financial

strife. This has been the case for generations. Alcoholism and financial bondage are diseases that have never been diagnosed as such in my family. And it wasn't until I acknowledged that we were all sick with these diseases and asked the Lord to heal us that we began to get well, that I began to get well.

All of my uncles and most of my aunts drank alcohol. "They go to bed with a drank and get up with and drank" was the old saying. My grandfather drank alcohol until the day he went home to be with the Lord. The same was true for most of the people in my family.

I grew up on a sprawling 42-acre farm. We always had food because we grew all our vegetables in our garden. Sweet potatoes, peanuts, corn, greens, and tomatoes were always on our table. And on the farm we raised cows, pigs, hogs, chickens, and mules. We also grew cotton and soybeans. We plowed and cultivated our fields, first with mules, then a tractor when we could afford it. We had several trees that produced good fruit: peach trees, pears trees, pecan trees, walnut trees, and figs trees.

When we wanted chicken we would go to the chicken house, catch one and slaughter it. When we wanted eggs, we would get some from the chicken house. If we wanted some beef, we slaughtered a young calf, and if we wanted some pork, we slaughtered a pig or a hog. If we wanted some fish, we went to the pond and caught some. If we wanted milk, we would milk the cows and make butter from the milk.

Yet with all of this abundance, we still struggled financially. I was the eighth of ten children, and things were always tight. We worked from sun up to sun down on the farm to make it prosperous, but we always ended at scratch. It was incredibly frustrating to always want more, but not having a clue what to do to get it... But thankfully, my mother did: she prayed.

My mother was a praying woman and she did not drink alcohol. We went to Church almost every Sunday. Our father would take us to church and pick us up after church services were over. My father never went to church (that I knew of), but he had a lot of the words of God in him. I believe my father learned God's word in school because they had the Bible in school when he was growing up.

I thank God there was never any violence in my family. The Hodges men love their family and most of their wives did not work. We believe in hard work and taking care of our families. There is no narcotic or drug addiction in my family. But alcoholism and financial oppression is rampant. Although my parents never spoke to us kids about their financial problems, I knew there were plenty, particularly once my mother got a job even after my father asked her not to.

When I found the Lord Jesus Christ and asked Him to come into my heart and be the Love over my life, the Lord delivered me from alcohol. The Lord also gave me a vision to be a baker and entrepreneur. I believe that the generational curse of alcoholism will be stop with me with the Lord's help. And I am praying that the spirit of alcoholism will be broken over my entire family. I am also praying that the spirit of financial bondage be broken over my entire family. We are working to see that through. Hallelujah!

    In learning to pray, I also learned the value of sharing my testimony. This book is a compilation of life lessons and God-insights that I gladly share in the hope that it blesses your life. Keep God at the forefront of your mind and at the center of your heart, and watch His glory shine in you!

Walking with God Through It All
David Hodges

Be Steadfast

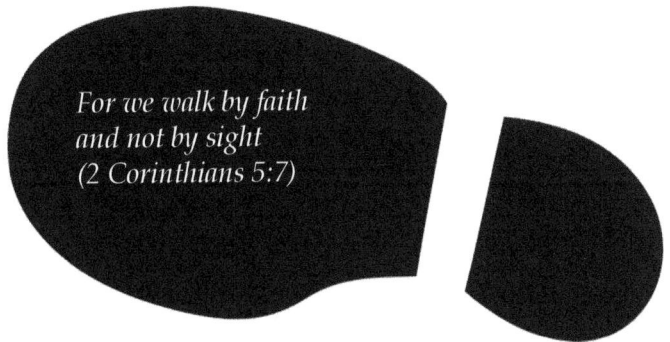

For we walk by faith and not by sight (2 Corinthians 5:7)

You must be steadfast in your belief and have faith in God's word. I live the word of God and put it into practice every day.

I decided to write a book. I didn't have all the funds necessary initially, but I trusted God to send me someone who would work with my budget. And He did. And although it was slow in the beginning, my patience paid off and I was able to complete the work I had started years ago and am now able to share my experiences with you.

God makes a way when we get busy and work through "it" – whatever "it" is!

Be Good Fruit

I abide in Christ, He abides in me and bear much fruit (John 15:5)

When you get saved, you invite Christ into your heart to live. He brings forth the fruit.

I pray a lot and I ask the Lord to allow my life experiences to be good examples for others to follow. I allow God to use me in any and every situation. I want to be Good Fruit.

One day when I was on the bus, the Lord told me to give this young man the "Father's Love Letter" by Father Heart Communications (I keep copies with me). The young man had been ranting about all the harm he was going to reign down on his boss the next day. When I gave the letter to the man, he read it in its entirety and said, "I'm not angry anymore."

It's possible that I prevented that young man from forever changing his life, the lives of his family, and his boss' life by some negative, harmful action - just by being obedient to God's voice.

Walking with God Through It All
David Hodges

Be Christ-Minded

I have the Mind of Christ and I hold the thoughts and purposes of his heart (1 Corinthians 2:16)

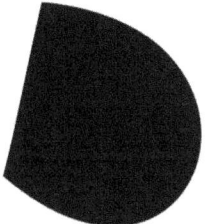

To have the mind of Christ, your mind must be renewed in him. Christ is His word. I purpose my heart to feed my mind with God's word every day.

I read my Bible and spend time with the Lord every day. I used to read the Bible every night, too, which I believe helped relieve the stress of the day and helped me to reflect on the good things that happened and release the bad. I believe that process was cleansing and renewing, and I am committed to starting it again.

Walking with God Through It All
David Hodges

Be Confident

I can do all things in Christ that strengthens me (Philippians 4:16)

Walking with God Through It All
David Hodges

I allow the Holy Spirit to strengthen me through prayer. It builds my spiritual muscles and fortifies my mind so when things go wrong I don't automatically go to bad thoughts and bad behaviors. I can focus on the good and how I may be of service to others.

I was diagnosed with Schizophrenia. I took the prescribed medicine, went to the hospital, went through therapy, but still felt that there was something missing. I asked the Lord to heal me, and through prayer and working with my doctors, I feel that I am on my way. I take my medicine, go to group therapy, study the Word, and pray every day for God to be with me. I believe He is. There was a time that I didn't think I would make it to see tomorrow. But now here I am by faith running my own baking business and now publishing my first book. God is good.

Walking with God Through It All
David Hodges

Be Courageous

No weapon formed against me shall prosper and every tongue that rise up against me in judgment shall be condemned. (Isaiah 54:17)

This is one of my favorite scriptures. I say it often and add "from the heels of my soul to the tip of my head" when I say it. Whenever I'm going through something, I feel the Lord working after I say this scripture.

My sister gave me this scripture when I got saved. She gave me two others, but this one really stuck out. This was over 40 years ago, in 1980. I was working on cruise ships, but stopped because my parents were having issues. I came home to help, but I didn't know what to do to help them save their marriage. I tried everything – including palm readers – but God kept me from that.

My sister gave me two places to go to for spiritual guidance. I was looking for truth, so I was very serious when evaluating where I would go. I called one place, and the pastor seemed to not believe what he preached. That wasn't for me. The second place was where I knew I needed to be. I went three times, and it was the third time that I came down the altar to receive the Lord and answer the call of discipleship. I didn't go back, because I was going to church with my sister at her church; but I got what I needed – my salvation was secure.

Walking with God Through It All
David Hodges

Be
In Love

I love the Lord God with all of my heart, soul and mind (Mark 12:30)

I say this scripture a lot, too. When I call the prayer line of a certain station and they ask my relationship with the Lord, I respond with this scripture. I believe this is key in my relationship with the Lord. You can't be lukewarm or cold when you're in love. You have to be on fire, and that's how I feel about the Lord.

People can tell I'm a man of God and that I walk with Him. My neighbors look out for me, watch over my home when I'm away, and I believe it's because they see God's light shining in me.

Walking with God Through It All
David Hodges

Be Loving

I love my neighbor as my myself (Mark 12:31)

I do love my neighbors, but neighbors aren't just people you live around, they're people you meet throughout your life experiences. Strangers are neighbors – if they have a need, try to meet it.

I ride the bus a lot, and when people ask me to pray with them, I do. When people behave in a way that's negative, I do what I can to correct them. That correction many times comes from me sharing my life experiences – the good, the bad, and the ugly.

Walking with God Through It All
David Hodges

Be Committed to Learning

I am the temple of the living God (2 Corinthians 6:16)

My inner man is the temple of the Holy Ghost because the Lord lives within me.

When I came to the Lord, I realized my life had changed. The teaching I was under taught me that my body was the temple of the Holy Spirit. It taught me to view myself as a new person in Christ. There were some aspects of myself that were child-like, that I was a baby and I needed to grow up in the spirit.

I started reading my Bible every morning when I awoke and in the evening before I went to bed. I began to understand the difference between spiritual and fleshly things. I committed to live a spiritually fulfilling life. That included going to church and learning the Word. I didn't get involved in activities so I wouldn't get distracted. I stayed focused on the Lord.

Walking with God Through It All
David Hodges

Be Obedient

I am faithful over a few things and I will be made ruler over many. (Matthew 25:23)

Whatever the Lord gives you to do, you need to do it. Start small so you may remain committed. Show the Lord He can trust you. As you get stronger in your faith, do bigger things.

Tithing is a good example. When you pay your tithes, you will notice your financial blessings grow. As you tithe more, your blessings grow, too. God knows He can trust you with more and therefore gives you more.

Walking with God Through It All
David Hodges

Be Steadfast

I submit to God, I resist the devil and he must flee from me. (James 4:7)

This is a scripture I quote frequently. When I'm going through things, and the enemy is attacking me, I turn to this scripture. If you submit to the Word of God, study His Word, and resist the devil, the enemy will stop and leave.

I've felt that I was living in a tunnel for 40 years. I'm just at the place where I can see. I sometimes say that I've been through the fire and I don't smell like smoke. That's what God has done for me – brought me through, knowing I went through something, but unscathed.

Walking with God Through It All
David Hodges

Be Focused

Greater is he that is in me than he that is in the world (1 John 4:4)

When I went through the tunnel, this scripture really brought me through. The Lord showed up and gave me peace in the midst of my struggles.

When I was wrestling with my calling to discipleship, I trusted the Lord to lead me to the right church to accept Christ, and again when He led me to the right church to actually join as a member.

My sister gave me this scripture when I felt fear as I left the first church. I knew that I was now part of the body of Christ, but wasn't sure what to do next. Once I focused on this scripture, God led me to the church that would become my church home.

Walking with God Through It All
David Hodges

Be Comforted

I am like a tree planted by the rivers of water and I bring forth fruit in my season. My leaf does not wither and whatever I do prospers (Psalm 1:3)

When you're planted in this world, you're planted by God. When you know you've been planted by God, you can be tossed and blown, but just like the palm tree, you bend but will not break no matter how life tries to beat you down.

In spite of my struggles that include mental illness and family division, I have not broken and will not be broken. God is with me. Life has taken me down all the way, but I got back up!

Walking with God Through It All
David Hodges

Be Honorable

My heart keeps the commandments of God, and length of days, long life, and peace shall they add unto me. (Proverbs 3:1-2)

Honor your parents and you will have long life. If you forgive others, you will have long life.

The Lord honors and forgives you.

When we commit to living the Word as it is written and not how we want things to be, God will place in our hearts contentment and satisfaction with life – and it shall be long and blessed.

Walking with God Through It All
David Hodges

Be Faithful

The Lord preserves my going out and my coming in from this time forth and forevermore (Psalm 121:8)

God protects His children.
As we go out during our days, working and running errands and just living; we must allow Him to lead us in all we do.

His protection and covering go with us no matter where we go, as long as we are living and going according to His word.

Walking with God Through It All
David Hodges

Be Willing to Change

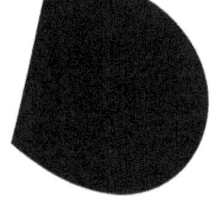

When I lie down, I will not be afraid and my sleep shall be sweet (Proverbs 3:24)

I remember praying this scripture over a woman who used to host our Saturday morning prayer meeting. She was having problems sleeping and she said that she hadn't realized that she wasn't where she should have been in her relationship with the Lord. She realized that she still had work to do in her relationships with others and the way she was living her life.

The realization of that gave her peace – she was able to ask God to humble her heart and show her how to change. That is how she was able to sleep, even before any work or actions had been done.

Be In Constant Search

I obtain favor of the Lord (Proverbs 12:2)

When you seek the Lord and look to Him for everything, He will give you favor – blessings, abundance, peace, joy, and love.

I sought the Lord when I knew I needed to change my life. It wasn't easy, but I had God's favor – favor in finding the right church, favor in finding the right prayer meeting, and favor in finding the right gatherings to lead me to write this book.

God's favor leads us to exactly where we are to be for the ultimate glory of Him.

Walking with God Through It All
David Hodges

Be Willing to Grow

I have all things freely through is son Jesus Christ who was delivered up for all (Romans 8:32)

Jesus has it all. He wants to give it to you.

When you seek Him and ask Him, He will give you the desires of your heart. He will whatever you need Him to do ... but you must grow in your walk with the Lord.

Receiving blessings of this magnitude requires spiritual maturity. That maturity is required to protect you from asking and receiving things too soon – or not in the right season. It also allows you to be a good steward over the tangible rewards and be a blessing to others with all that Jesus gives.

Walking with God Through It All
David Hodges

Be Merciful

Surely goodness and mercy shall follow me all the days of my life and I will dwell in the house of the Lord forever (Psalm 23:6)

Once you come to the Lord and commit to His ways and obey Him, then no matter what life tosses at you, mercy shall be on the other side.

Sometimes it takes time to get through it. Life can be tough. But God is tougher. He made life and He made you strong enough to endure and overcome all. With God, all things are possible.

When my parents divorced and wouldn't tell me why, it took me to a dark place. But on the other side of darkness was God's light. God's mercy. God's goodness. And it wasn't easy, but it was doable. And I'm stronger for it all.

Walking with God Through It All
David Hodges

Be Accountable

The Lord shall decree a thing, and it shall be established unto me and light shall shine upon my ways (Job 22:28)

Whatever God called you to do, you need to do it. The world calls us to do many things – some according to our gifts, others according to our financial desires.

It's important not to be pulled off the path that God has set. We know what the path is because it feels right – God's peace rests in our hearts. We know it's right because no matter how we try to stray from it, God keeps bringing it back into our lives.

God holds us accountable for all the gifts He places within us, and He knows when we are turning away from responsibilities to others that the gifts were given to us to serve.

Walking with God Through It All
David Hodges

Be Ready

I am taught of the Lord's ways and I walk in his paths (Isaiah 2:3)

The Holy Spirit is our teacher. He teaches us as we read and study God's word. This allows the Holy Spirit to lead and guide us in all we do. He is a beacon as we walk our life path, keeping us out of harm. But we must live according to God's word.

When I committed to studying God's word night and day so I could grow, I was showing God I wanted to learn his ways and be obedient to His word. I was showing Him that I could be trusted with whatever He gave me. And I was showing Him I was ready for more.

Walking with God Through It All
David Hodges

Be Wise

I know that the Son of God is come and have given me an understanding that I may know him that is true (1 John 5:20)

I have been a member of my current church for some time and have been happy. But I have learned that when the Lord speaks, I must obey. I have also learned that God does not mind when I ask for confirmation that the instructions that I believe came from Him actually did. And so when I felt that the Lord was leading me to return to a former congregation, I asked for confirmation that it was in fact God sending me back.

I visited the church and also made plans to attend prayer meeting. I realized how much I had grown since I'd left my former church family: before I had suffered and wrestled with a spirit that did not allow me to accept or receive help from others. The pastor there once said to me, "David, you're going to die like this."

Since I've been away, I have learned to accept and receive help, and to ask for it as well. And I believe that may be a reason God is telling me to return.

Be Truthful

Behold you desire the truth in the inward parts, and in the hidden part you shall make me to know wisdom (Psalm 51:6)

Walking with God Through It All
David Hodges

Before I was saved, I always sought truth. It was this seeking that opened me to being saved. God plants in fertile ground. One's mind is the ground. God will not plant until that ground is receptive and able to yield good fruit.

Truth makes the ground fertile. Once my mind was prepared for the planting, God seeded into me and those seeds took root, allowing the Holy Spirit to enter and grow. As the Spirit grew in me, my mind was renewed. And I was able to see my way through the struggle and strife my life had become.

It was hard, but with the help of the people God sent my way, including my sister who took me to her church, and the church families I have experienced along the way, I am a living witness of all that God can and will do if we seek first His truth and the Kingdom of God.

Walking with God Through It All
David Hodges

Be A Disciple

I am not ashamed of the Gospel of Christ (Romans 1:6)

I talk about God where ever I go. Because I am talking about Him and sharing His word, I can talk to anybody on any level. God puts the words in my mouth that people need to hear.

One day I was riding the bus and this very angry young man was cursing up a storm. Because of my struggles, I knew what was wrong with him. A demon had him and he was in need of prayer. God told me to start talking to him, but before I could get in good, the man moved away from me. When I asked why, he told me he could feel the anointing on me, that the Spirit was that strong. I still shared the gospel with him, and he calmed immediately.

When you are strong enough to remove yourself from the situation and put forth the God in you, He will take over and minister to His people as they need.

Walking with God Through It All
David Hodges

Be Loyal

I desire the sincere milk of the Word that I may grow thereby
(1 Peter 2:2)

The Word of God nourishes every inch of the body, mind, and soul. Reading the Word daily builds the mind, which tells the body what to do, and the soul is fortified to deal with whatever comes to us day to day.

I remember seeing this in action in January 1999 when I met one of God's angels. The angel took the form of a man, and had the voice of my father (who was living at the time). The angel asked me, "When are you going to turn back from the Lord?" and challenged me for about five minutes until I said, "I live this gospel".

Although I had gotten saved in 1980, the Lord started really dealing with me and the calling He had on my life in 1999. This was the beginning of that journey.

Later that night as I was deep in my prayers, I remember hearing the Lord's voice say, "You know that was an angel," and I was stunned. But also pleased because I felt like I had pleased the Lord in my response.

I was not and am not a perfect man. I've make my mistakes, but knowing that God cares so much for me that He sent an angel to ensure that I knew where my help came from, made and makes me feel so special and loved.

Be Loveable

Faith, hope and love (especially love) abide in me (1 Corinthians 13:13)

Love is everything about the Bible, everything about our Christian walk. If we have faith, hope, and love, we can move mountains. My pastor used to say, "If you love God, you'll love people."

It's an agape love, a full and encompassing love, above and beyond us. It allows God to fight our battles, allows us to forgive the unforgiveable, and teaches us to move beyond our perceived limitations.

Walking with God Through It All
David Hodges

Be Righteous

I am the seed of Abraham and just like him, God has counted me righteous (Genesis 15:6)

We must live what we know. We know from the Word that we were made in God's image. That means He made us like Him physically and spiritually. And even when we succumb to the worldly temptations that are placed in front of us every day, we still have God in us.

At any point we may make the choice to embrace that God in us.

Walking with God Through It All
David Hodges

Be Humble

I am meek and inherit the earth (Matthew 5:5)

We cannot receive the physical earth, but we can receive the spiritual connection of all of God's creations. When we humble ourselves and open ourselves to loving each person we meet, we share God's love and receive it too. That openness allows us to inherit God's grace, mercy, peace, joy, and love.

Walking with God Through It All
David Hodges

Be A Praying Warrior

I will pray for all those in authority over me that I may lead a quiet and peaceful life in all godliness and honesty (1Timothy 2:2)

I always pray for the people who lead me. It's important, whether I like them or not, that they know that there is someone who wants God to protect them, lead them, and love them.

I pray for my leaders as if I am praying for myself, asking God to give them wisdom and discernment, and to make good decisions so that all our lives are positively impacted.

Walking with God Through It All
David Hodges

Be An Evangelist

I have been given the power to become a child of God (John 1:12)

When we accept Christ as our Lord and Savior, we become a member of the body of Christ. That means that we have access to the power that gave Christ His power and authority to heal, to make things plain with wisdom, and to build others up. We also obtain a direct source to God. Knowing that also gives us responsibility to preach the Gospel and to stand on God's Word.

When I was in Honolulu, I remember telling someone that I was a pastor. I was walking home from church, but I was the pastor of that church. To be clear, I did not and had not pastored any church, but the words came from my mouth. I believe it was because as a member of the body of Christ, I know that I have the same responsibility to share the Word of the Lord as a pastor of a physical building. I also have responsibility to teach others how to share God's Word and to comfort the flock.

I don't have a building where I come to preach every Sunday. I preach and share the joy of the Lord wherever I am. It's not a street ministry per se, but a "wherever I am" ministry.

Walking with God Through It All
David Hodges

Be
Unencumbered

I seek first the Kingdom and God's righteousness, and all things will be added unto me (Matthew 6:33)

I use this scripture to pray over others, so that they stay focused on what's important in life: getting into Heaven. It's important not to be distracted by worldly possession and wealth because they come and they go. But God's love is eternal and it is the only thing we can really rely on.

Walking with God Through It All
David Hodges

Be Worshipful

I am a true worshiper, one who worships in spirit and in truth (John 4:23)

I believe in truth. Truth and worship go hand in hand. Truth allows you to take your worship to a higher level. It allows you to see life for what it is and ask God for direction.

We stop trying to hide our imperfections (like God doesn't see them anyway!) and ask Him to heal us, direct us, and to be a beacon of light to others.

Walking with God Through It All
David Hodges

Be Grounded

I do not live off bread alone, but of every word that proceeds from the mouth of God (Deuteronomy 8:3)

When I was going through the hardest times of my life, I turned to this scripture. It kept me grounded, and helped me to banish thoughts from my mind that were not Godly.

Food is necessary for the body, but spiritual fruits are necessary for the soul.

Walking with God Through It All
David Hodges

Be Alive

Out of my belly flows rivers of living water (John 7:37)

When you're praying in the spirit, i.e., praying in tongues, it's like rivers of water flowing up and through you. You will say and think things that you KNOW did not form in your own mind – these thoughts and words are directly from God.

These inspirations and insights allow you to minister to others, be successful in your business, love your family through hard times, and be patient and loving to yourself.

Embrace the flow of the living water. Bathe in it and share the passion with others.

Be Selected

I have been chosen by God to bring forth fruit that shall remain (John 15:16)

I believe we are all chosen by God – once we are saved. We are called to the Kingdom by the preaching of the Word, and are selected once we accept the call to discipleship. We have unique gifts and abilities that are to be used for God's glory. These gifts and abilities differentiate us from nonbelievers. Not to hurt or to condemn, but to heal and to lift up and bring to God's holy will.

Be Renewed

I am a brand new person inside, pure and holy full of God's goodness (1 Corinthians 1:30 and 2 Corinthians 5:17, 5:21)

When we talk to our Inner Man, God can come in.

Once we are saved, we are renewed, becoming brand new in Christ. It gives us the pureness of who we really are, allowing us to share this joy and understanding with others. People see the light shining in us and want to know where it comes from. It's at that moment that we must share the Holy love and peace that being in God's will has brought to us. That is how we win souls to Christ.

Walking with God Through It All
David Hodges

Be Released

My sins have been taken away and I am now chosen, adopted and forgiven with every spiritual blessing in heavenly places (Ephesians 1:7, 1:3)

Once we come into Christ, adopted into His Kingdom, we are forgiven of all sins and we receive our blessings. We are released from meanness if we wish it, unforgiveness if we wish it, and doubt if we wish it.

God can relieve our minds of every burden, our heart of every hurt, and our body of every pain – but only if we trust and believe.

Walking with God Through It All
David Hodges

Be Healed

I am free from sickness, I believe in my heat that Jesus wounds heal me. I can lay my hand on the sick and will recover (1 Peter 2:24, Mark 16:18)

Get into the habit of laying hands on yourself. Say, "I'm a believer. I lay hands on myself, and I believe that I shall recover." Whatever pain I'm in usually goes away when I do this. We won't always have someone else around to do this for us, so it's important that we turn to God and learn to pray healing and blessings over ourselves.

It's by faith that we receive our healing.

Be More

I have everything because I have Christ and I am filled with God (Colossians 2:10)

We receive more as we grow in Christ. God is able to share with us more knowledge, more wisdom, more love, more power – more everything! God knows that He can trust us with more when we use what He has already given us to seed into others.

God will never give us more than we can bear. Therefore, when we give to others, it frees us so that God may give us more of him.

Walking with God Through It All
David Hodges

Be Forgiving

Whatever I ask for in prayer, I believe that I have received it (Mark 11:24)

Everything you ask for, you will receive it – once you forgive.

Unforgiveness is a burden – it's something you hold. God can't give you more until you release those things that take up room in your life.

God can't for-GIVE until you GIVE up hard thoughts, mean ways, and selfishness.

Remember, God doesn't give us more than we can bear – bear as in hold, use wisely, be loving, and share with others to his edification.

Walking with God Through It All
David Hodges

Be Subservient

I am part of a chosen generation, a royal priesthood, and a holy nation. I am one of God's own people. (1 peter 2:9)

Jesus is our King. Once we accept Him as our savior, we become part of His inner circle, a priest ordained by the Holy Spirit. With priesthood comes status and responsibility; acceptance and direction; love and call to action.

Being a member of God's circle, one of His special designees, is a privilege and honor that should not be taken lightly.

The charge to share God's Word must be taken seriously.

Be Discerning

I am not fearful because God has given me the spirit of power, love and self-control (2 Timothy 1:7)

There was fear in me, even after I accepted the call. It was not released until I attended a revival where Juanita Bynum was the keynote. I didn't even know there was fear in me until I said, "You'll be dead or in jail." They were words spoken over me at a previous church by an elder in that church. I was deeply wounded by those words because I was a new believer, working hard to prove myself worthy of the King. I didn't fully understand that there was nothing to prove – Jesus' sacrifice on the cross had removed the need to "show and prove". All I needed to do was to believe and share that belief with others. Once I said the words that had unknowingly bound me, I was released and freed to embrace the fullness of God's love. We must be careful what we say to others AND what we accept that others say about us.

Be Born Again

I am a citizen of God's Kingdom and member of his household (Ephesians 2:19)

Once we are born again, we get a whole new life – we become part of a new country, the Kingdom of God. We become part of a new family – the family of believers. We live in a new house – God's house. And the love that flows from this newness is infinite – it will last forever. AND we get to bring people over and hang out with them at any time in our new country, in our new house, with our new family! Can you image a family that keeps growing, one full of love and happiness, and peace, and joy? One that has no lack, no pain, no unforgiveness, and no strife?

This is God's Kingdom, this is His household. And it is waiting for you!

Walking with God Through It All
David Hodges

Be Decisive

In Christ I was chosen before the world was made, in his love he chose me to be a holy person and without blame before him (Ephesians 1:4)

Before God made the world, He knew who was going to be in it. He knew who would accept his call and who would not. He knew what each person – you included – would do with the opportunity to be part of His Kingdom. And even knowing this, He still gave every person – and still gives every person – the opportunity to make his/her own choice.

God doesn't force his will on anyone. His love is so vast that he allows us to decide what we want out of life, how we're going to live it, and gives us countless opportunities to join him.

God is love personified.

Be Trusting

I trust and believe in Christ, I have been sealed with the Holy Spirit of promise the deposit of my inheritance (Ephesians 1:13)

Once we are called, we must trust God to give us the Holy Spirit. The Holy Spirit is a promise of the inheritance – the Kingdom of God. The Holy Spirit is peace, joy, and love. It is everything that is good and right. And once we accept the Holy Spirit into our hearts, the wonder of the Lord resides in us all ways – and in all ways – ready to direct us, lead us, guide us, and help us in every area of our lives. We must just ask and it shall be.

Walking with God Through It All
David Hodges

Be Pure

In Christ Jesus, I have been made a new person that I may do the good works he has planned for me (Ephesians 2:10)

Once we accept Jesus into our hearts and lives, we are molded into a new person – the best version of our selves possible.

Good works don't do it – it must be a change of heart. The change of heart directs our thoughts and actions. The thought behind our actions must be pure and full of love. These things are what we must strive for in this life. A mind renewed by God's love.

Be Excited

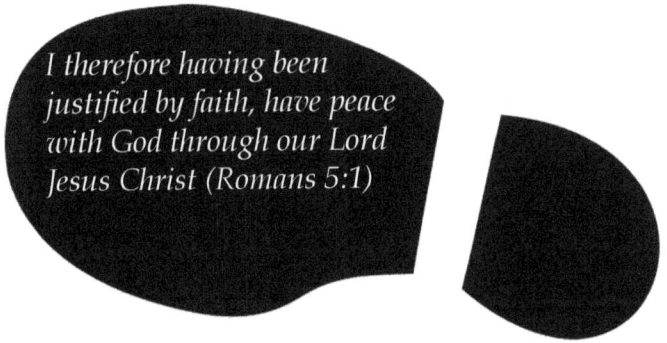

Sometimes we have "the opportunity" before we are ready to fully appreciate it.

I recently rejoined a previous church and am now able to fully appreciate all that it has for me. I am excited about what is to come in my life, excited about what God is doing and is about to do using me. This book is just one thing that God is using for me to help share His word with others.

I am humbled and in deep prayer about how I may continue to grow in the Lord.

Be Fixable

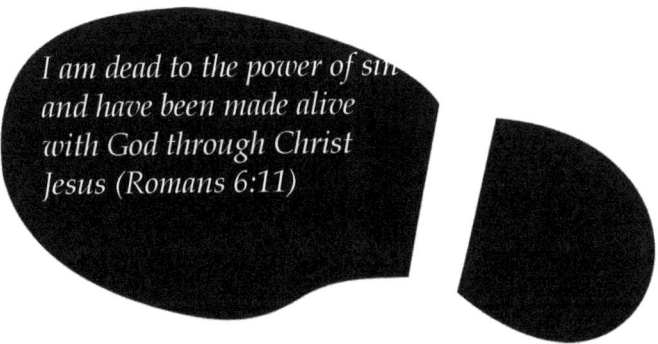

I am dead to the power of sin and have been made alive with God through Christ Jesus (Romans 6:11)

God prepares us to do His work.

Sometimes that means refining us through several processes and "repair shops". God has done so in my life. I have been blessed to be ministered to by great men and women of God. My first repair shop or church was tasked with removing the spirits that tormented me. The next process was completed by a more specialized repair shop that fitted me with my particular spiritual gifts that include praying (or being a prayer warrior) and evangelism (sharing my testimony with others). I was then led to another repair shop that allowed me to grow in my relationship with God. And now I am in a place where I can help others go through their process in being disciples of the Lord.

To be in a place where I could see that I needed to move and to grow required me to forgive others and myself. Without forgiveness, there is pain and suffering, guilt and blame – none of these things are of God. They are negative and drain the life out of you. That prevents you from being all that God wants you to be in Him: a warrior and a conqueror for Christ!

Walking with God Through It All
David Hodges

Be Introspective

I have redemption through his blood and the forgiveness of sins according to the riches of his grace (Ephesians 1:7)

My parents had a difficult relationship, and unfortunately, I as a child was a witness to it and was hurt by it.

When I was three, my older brothers asked me what I wanted to be when I grew up. My dad was coming home from work, I saw him, and not knowing what to say, I said, "I want to be like my daddy!" My mother overhead it – but at the time, I thought that it was my brothers who told her about my innocent statement. From that moment, my mother shunned me. It was not until later in life – I was about 24 – when I shared my pain with a chaplain who had similar difficulties in his family that I came to realize how much unforgiveness was in my heart. That chaplain helped me to see that I must forgive my mother for shunning me, my father for being a person that my mother did not like – so much so that she would mistreat her child for simply saying he wanted to be like his dad, and I had to forgive myself for feeling that it was my fault.

I also realized the unreasonable anger I had with my older brother – I was convinced that he had set me up for this pain, but he too was only a child when all this transpired and could not have known the far reaching consequences of his question.

It was God that allowed me to see the pain and suffering that existed in my parents' relationship. It was God that allowed me to forgive and pray for both of them to be healed and made whole. And it was God that allowed me the strength to tell this story so that someone reading it may know that they are precious and perfect in God's love.

Be Royal

I have been raised with Christ and sit with him in the heavenly places (Ephesians 2:6)

When you are saved, there is no other place for you to sit but with Christ, and He sits in the heavenly kingdom. So therefore you sit in the Kingdom!

Be Delighted

> *I am the light of the world. I am like a city on top of a hill that cannot be hidden (Matthew 5:14)*

When I am praying for people, I know that I am a light in the world. I am standing in the gap, pulling souls to Christ. It is a marvelous feeling! And I am so grateful and humbled that God allows me to do it every day!

It is a great feeling when people I have prayed with or prayed for come to me later and say, "You're the one who brought me in!" I rejoice to the depths of my soul!

Walking with God Through It All
David Hodges

Be Delivered

I shall not be afraid because the Lord is my light, my salvation, and the strength of my life (Psalm 27:1)

Walking with God Through It All
David Hodges

I have had a lot of challenges. I remember a time when I was still of the world, but knew I needed… something. I would walk to this one church seven miles to catch the bus to get there because I believed that they could help me. They had a deliverance ministry, so surely they could help little old me. But what I needed they could not provide. They were very generous – they offered me clothes, food, and a place to stay. I had all of these things. They assumed I needed these physical comforts because I chose to walk seven miles and catch a bus. (Looking back, what they should have offered was a car! But I digress.) What I needed was to be delivered from the demons that plagued me. The doubt, fear, and unforgiveness that were in my heart. These were things that only God could remove.

And after searching many more weeks, I found a church that had a prayer warrior at the helm who showed me how to pray and ask the Lord to deliver me. And He did! Halleluiah!

Be Dutiful

I am bold as a lion because Jesus has made me the righteous of God (Proverbs 28:1)

Walking with God Through It All
David Hodges

Sometimes you have to walk a long way to get to where God needs you to be to grow in Him and to minister to his flock. I walked 22 miles once to see a very prominent TV minister. She was incredible and totally worth every step. I thought that the reason God had me come was just for me. But as God does, He accomplishes many things with one action.

I received a mighty blessing from the words spoken that night. Really, I got a heart full within the first five minutes. I was doubly blessed to be in the presence of that minister not too long after. And when I tried to share what God put on my heart for her to hear, she shut me out. She wasn't rude, but you know when someone isn't receiving what you are saying. At first I felt defeated because I couldn't image why God would set me up with this wonderful woman to share His message of glory for her life if she wasn't going to hear it. But He whispered quietly to me that it wasn't me she was rejecting – I reminded her too much of her ex-husband. Now, I didn't look like him, but something about me triggered in her a remembrance of him and it was too uncanny.

That will happen when we minister to others. But we cannot let the fact that people chose not to hear us deter us from doing what God had us to do. Although that minister didn't receive what I said at that moment, it's a real possibility that later on she prayed on my words and took them to heart. It isn't for me to know, rather it is for me to obey.

Be Blessed

My hope is in the Lord and I will be blessed. I am like a tree planted by the water my roots are large and will find water and I shall never cease to bear fruit (Jeremiah 17:7)

I am grounded in my work. By being into the Word, I am able to allow the Word to come alive in me through everything I do. I know that whatever it is I do in the Lord will be blessed. Those blessing may be material things, good friendships, new business opportunities, a spiritual awakening, or seeing a new beautiful flower I'd never noticed before. But in all these things I will be blessed.

Be Graceful

> The Lord gives me grace and glory. I will walk upright before him and he will withhold no good thing from me (Psalms 84:11)

Walking with God Through It All
David Hodges

I don't know where I'd be but for the grace of God. I lived before I was saved, but I became alive when I accepted Jesus into my heart. I now know that all things work to God's good and glory – the good times and the bad times in my life. And now I know that I am never alone, no matter what.

Be Refined

Jesus Christ is my Lord and Savior and I will do the works that Jesus did (John 14:12)

Sometimes the Lord my remove us from a place because we're not ready to receive our blessings or the work that comes with them.

I remember being part of a ministry that I knew in my soul was where I was supposed to be. But I needed to have more experiences and further develop my evangelism and discipleship gifts. Once those were at a place where God could use me effectively, He returned me to that ministry. And now instead of fighting the leaders, I am humble and excited about the instruction that I am to receive.

Be Watchful

Whatever I ask in the name of Jesus, He will do it for me so that God may be glorified (John 14:12)

I see God in every little thing, big and small.

There was a popular minister who used to praise God when he stumped his toe! I remembered thinking that he was crazy. But when you're living this thing, and have God in your heart, you really see Him in every thing – every action, every person, every pain, every sorrow, every joy, and every healing. God IS glorified in everything we do.

Be Saved

I have been saved God's grace and I confess with my mouth that Jesus is my Savior and Lord (Ephesians 2:5, Romans 10:9)

Being saved by grace is the foundational scripture for Salvation. I've brought many new believers to the Lord by praying this prayer over them. In speaking the confession, we denounce Satan and his hold over us. It is through these words that we acknowledge God's total power over us and our destiny. And it is good!

Walking with God Through It All
David Hodges

Be Generous

In Christ I have become a child of God and I receive the blessings God has for me
(John 1:12, Romans 16:17)

I am just now beginning to receive the blessings God has for my life. It's exciting to know there is more to come because I feel so full now – and it's only the beginning! I am excited to share my talents and the word of God with others. And to know that in sharing that I will receive abundance thrills my soul!

Walking with God Through It All
David Hodges

Be Wonder Full

In Christ God has chosen me as his own and made me strong. God has placed his mark on me. He has placed his spirit in my heart as a guarantee for all he has promised (2 Corinthians 1:14)

When I received my calling, I didn't know how to go about accepting my appointment. I knew God was with me and that as long as I walked according to His Word, that I would find my way.

I saw pastors who were under the calling of other pastors and knew that wasn't for me. I saw evangelists working in the community, and knew that wasn't quite it either. But in watching and talking and working with and alongside all of these blessed people, I was doing exactly what God wanted me to do. The more experiences I had, the more effective my testimony would be. And I now enjoy and understand the purpose of the journey to my ultimate calling. And I once again wonder at God's holy ability to use everything for His good – even my indecision!

Walking with God Through It All
David Hodges

Be Victorious

In Christ God has given me the victory, and he uses me to spread his knowledge everywhere (2 Corinthians 1:14)

We are in this world, but not of it. We have ultimate victory in Christ through everything that we go through. We have an opportunity every day to be a bright light, a beacon, for others who are searching for answers to all this world throws at them.

We move forward knowing that no matter what comes our way, we are not alone. We have all that we need and are armed with God's power and authority.

Walking with God Through It All
David Hodges

Be Vigilant

I am healed and delivered from sin because Christ was wounded for the wrong I did, healed because of His wounds (Isaiah 53:5-7, I Peter 2:24)

It's not people, it's the enemy, that keeps bringing up the bad stuff in your life.

When you are reminded of the person you used to be, it is the enemy testing your new commitment to God and His holy work. Don't be mad at the person reminding you, instead rebuke the devil and keep moving. Through Jesus' stripes, you are healed. Not some people, all people – including you and the person who the devil used to try to drag you back. Pray for that person and know that God is praying for you!

Walking with God Through It All
David Hodges

Be God's Child

I can do all things in Christ that strengthens me (Philippians 4:24)

Walking with God Through It All
David Hodges

I live this scripture. If not for the truth in it, I don't know where I'd be – definitely not in my right mind. God has blessed me: He has kept me through illness, mental instability, family strife, homelessness, joblessness, loneliness, isolation, depression, and every bad thing that could have happened, but didn't. And I know it was all for God's ultimate glory and for my good.

Walking with God Through It All
David Hodges

Prayer of Salvation

That if you confess with your mouth the Lord Jesus and believe in your heart that God has raised him from the dead, you will be saved. (Romans 10:9)

Jesus, I ask you to forgive me of all my sins and wash me clean with your blood. I ask you to come into my heart and be the Lord of my life. I denounce Satan, and recognize you Jesus as Lord of my life from this day forward. In Jesus name! Amen.

Your salvation will come alive when you tell someone.

About the Author

The eighth child in a family of ten, David Hodges was always considered a "go-getter". He never took "no" for an answer and always had a desire to learn more and more.

David was born in Lexington, Mississippi and grew up on a sprawling 42-acre farm. He was always fascinated with baking and spent hours in the kitchen watching his mother bake. One day when David was ten years old, as he sat in the kitchen watching his mother kneading dough, a love came over him to bake, and that is when he knew that he, too, would one day grow up to be a baker.

At the age of fifteen, David began to dream of going around the world working as a baker and his dream was to do it on the waters. As he pursued his dream, even through High School and on to Atterbury Job Corps Center in Edinburg, Indiana; David enrolled in a Baker's Class and graduated with a diploma in baking.

The vision from so long ago had now sprouted wings, and David was off and running in pursuit of his dream. From Atterbury, he went on to Chicago and worked for Ward Bakery for three months. Form there David and his brother left Chicago and headed cross-county in a 1967 Nova and ended up in Los Angeles. There he enrolled in Central Adult School and took a course in Cake Decorating, graduating in the top half of his class. Still hungering and thirsting for more knowledge, David enrolled in a baking and cooking course at the Clarified Job Corps Center in Oregon, Utah and walked right into his destiny.

One of David's teachers asked if any of the students wanted to go into the Merchants Marines. The job entailed traveling around the world working on cruise ships. Of courses David jumped at the chance and enrolled in Marine Cooks and Stewards School in Santa Rosa California where he took more baking and cake decorating courses. Soon David graduated and was off to the "high seas." He worked on a variety of cruise ships as a cook and baker for a number of years.

After David's parents separated, he had a breakdown and resigned from the Merchants Marines. He went home and searched for answers to life's great questions while going through treatment for Schizophrenia and depression.

David accepted the Lord Jesus Christ into his heart on May 5, 1980. The pastor's message that day was on Jesus' as our eternal life line. This led David to the MasterLife books because he want to know who is a disciple and how to become one.

After much study, David was moved to share his life story so that others would be brought to the Word of God and saved by Jesus' grace and mercy.

www.ingramcontent.com/pod-product-compliance
Lightning Source LLC
Chambersburg PA
CBHW051102160426
43193CB00010B/1288